whispers overheard

bernadette glover

PRESS

May 6, 2012

Sis Gretchen,

May the love of God
blanket your life.

Dedication

To My Parents

Anna L. Glover, tenacious and gracious, for always believing in me. Reverend Sterling Glover, innovative and challenging, for assuring that my best is good enough. Thanks for everything!

Heritage

Dear Lord, kind Lord unto
thee I pray look down upon
thy people raging in
bloody conflict today
look down upon thy
people of every nation,
every color, every creed.
And, fill them with thy
spirit for that is what they
need.
Anna L. Glover – 1948

Our battle in this 21st century is not between materialism, secularism and humanism, but the deeper struggle between cynicism and hope!! Faith does not step over these issues into a heavenly utopia. But faith can follow the trail of that lonely Nazarene through invisible walls of demonic defeatism. It is only in following the Christ of God, whom God raised from suffering and death and from the grave it gains an open prospect in which there is nothing more to oppress us, there's a view of the realm of freedom and joy.
Rev. Sterling E. Glover – 2008

Introduction

Who are our best story tellers? "Big Mothers" in the Ghanaian marketplace? Southern preachers from the US milieu? Grandmothers and grandfathers from every culture who know how to please and to tantalize with the words, "Once upon a time?" There was a man in the Middle East who told stories beginning with, "There was once a rich man. . . or a poor woman. . . or a father with two sons." He may have been the best storyteller of all. We still repeat his tales and wonder at their meaning.

As wonder we must. Good stories draw us because they refuse to give themselves away. They tantalize and suggest, but don't tell all. We are invited into the space they leave for us. We walk among the words, looking for clues, and asking our questions? Was Helen worth a ten years war? What *was* Alice seeking in that mirror? What if Scheherazade had not awakened one fine morning to seduce the king with mysteries? Did the older brother join the prodigal's party after all?

The stories you are about to read are enigmas. They tease the heart and mind. They suggest and run away. They want you to play. Seek and you shall find. The writer has a sparkle in her eye, a deep laugh, and wisdom gathered from many places and teachers.

Take your time on the journey. Double back for a second read. Don't ever think you've gathered it all. More awaits. Once upon a time. . . .

Betsy Morgan

Awakening

Two sided coins …
admiration/envy,
strength/weakness
Regardless of which side
is up (virtue or vice)
handle with humility – a
coin flips with far too
great ease.

The Score

The chimes sounded… Seeing the "Petals to Please" truck outside, the door opens gladly with a smile. Interviews, cameras, a high-five here, there were becoming the norm for a legend in the making.

"Is this the Bounds' residence?" A rather timid young man asked.

"That's what the sign says." was the smirk reply.

"I've got a delivery for Coach Bounds. I'll, I'll be right back." The young man scurried to his vehicle, leaving the coach scanning for a spot to the arrangement. Congratulations of all sorts littered the foyer and just about everywhere. Hearing a faint tap coach turned from triumphant salutations back to the door.

"Wrong house. Wrong house. WRONG HOUSE!" coach blared. "Find a funeral, a cemetery or something. First, you can't read. Now, you can't think. Nobody would bring that here. Nobody!" SLAM! The door was shut and both coach's slippers were hurled at it in a huff.

He fumed: "Dumber by the day. These delivery people, these kids just get dumber… wait! What am I talking about? It's not the young man, it's who sent the flowers…."

"Hey! Hey!" Coach hollered, as he snatched the door. The young man was gone, but not the delivery. A large bleeding heart with a "Beloved Coach" ribbon stood eye to eye with Bounds. The attached card read: "In Almost Loving Memory. Coach, the power of life and death are in the tongue. You're in ICU. We're in emergency. All of us need life support. – The Team." With trophies in peripheral view, the emerging legend stared at the card in his bone dry hand. He thought to himself: "losing a team while winning a season, is that what's been going on?"

The Mirror

The phone was so hot it blistered the hand that tried to hold it. The caller's voice scorched through and angrily ignited the whole room. "You call this a house? This isn't fit for a roach! I thought you knew my standards. After all these years, you above all people should have known that this - Have you actually seen this place? What fool convinced you that this dump would be suitable for me?"

"Mr. Wright, let me explain."

"Explain?" He snapped. "There's nothing to explain. I'm not finished! In fact, when I'm ready to hear what you've got to say, I'll let you know. You hear me?"

"Yes sir."

"A nice quiet spot where I could relax, reflect is what I asked for. A place where I could pray. I even said I wanted to work on myself, didn't I?"

"You did."

"Of course I did …and you send me here? The wood isn't polished, glass isn't glistening, even the door knobs are dull. Everything is dull, lifeless. There isn't a shine to be seen anywhere. This is an insult, totally unacceptable. You should have never been hired in the first place. I was talked into it. Pack your things. Clean out your desk. Someone competent who can be trusted to carry out directives in light of my stature is needed. You're not it. *You* are *not* the one. Now say something."

"How do you like the view?"

"In this run down mansion?"

"How do you like the view Mr. Wright? (Calmly spoken).
Aren't you on a small hill with a little lake not far off?"

"If I could see out of these dirty windows I might have an answer," he snapped. "Didn't I tell you to clean out your desk?"

"Yes, and I'm doing it as were talking."

"You're interrupting my conversation with cleaning? Why don't you send someone to clean here?...And yes, the hill and lake are here. They're beautiful. Everything was very peaceful until I made the mistake of going inside. And where are the mirrors? Who builds a house, decorates a house, and rents a house that has no mirrors?"

"Since I'm already fired Mr. Wright, please let me explain…"

"Tell my driver. Your actions have said it all." A door slammed loudly and the driver got on the phone.

"Jasmine, what happened? Mr. Wright is furious and then some. He's been ranting and raving ever since we came inside. This house is *really* nice but he's gone from room to room opening and closing this and that. The furniture is gorgeous with no dust, no dirt in sight. There's some type of smell here that seems to be everywhere. I guess you call it an aroma. Whatever it is, it's coming through the vents. And soft music is playing. You know the kind that makes the weight of the world melt. I like it here myself. It is different though- without mirrors; but, I like it."

"It sounds like everything is the way it's supposed to be, Jasmine replied. Greg, look on the table in the foyer. There should be a card with Mr. Wright's name on it."

"Got it."

"Give it to Mr. Wright. If he doesn't open it, then would you open it and read it to him? Make sure he reads the card Greg."

"Ok Jasmine. But what if he…"

"I know. Trust me. It will all make sense after he's read the card."

Mr. Wright was still shaking his head in disbelief, mumbling "how could she, how could they put me in a place like this. Someone put them up to this. I'll find out."

Greg walked over to Mr. Wright and extended the card. "I know you're mad and probably through with more than Jasmine, but she said this card will spell everything out. Mr. Wright snatched it and tore into something he had no idea was coming."

The card read:

Dear Mr. Wright,

You said you wanted to go where you could relax, reflect and be at home. Well, here it is. Because you don't reflect on yourself, all the mirrors were removed. Objects that offered a possibility of reflection were left without a shine. The choice of locations, amenities were made with your comfort in mind. But who you are is more than you think.

Jasmine

A silent Mr. Wright went over to the French doors that led to the veranda. After standing there trying to command the lump in his throat to move for almost an hour, he went outside. Waving Greg off who was calling after him – "Are we staying? Are we going? Are you okay?" Mr. Wright responded in a civil tone "never mind Greg. Never mind. Give me a minute, please."

Three hours later Greg's phone rang. It was Jasmine. "How's he doing Greg?"

"I'm not sure Jaz; he's still by the lake trying to see himself."

The Twins

They went back and forth, off and on, for weeks. Exhausted by the relentless posturing of first this and then that one, the OB-GYN's words were a relief. So it was, on Wednesday February 29, Dr. Another Default Choice fostered the birthing of a set of twins. Just as it had taken forever for the babies to arrive, it took forever for Mr. and Mrs. All Right to name them. After much discussion and conferring with family and friends, they finally agreed. Both children will have "Doing" as a first name in honor of a stillborn sibling. "Is" would be their middle name since the All Rights understood themselves to have a reality based orientation to life. So with Doing Anything Is All Right and Doing Nothing Is All Right in their arms, the couple returned to their home nestled on Dilemmas Drive in the village of Whatever.

Although initially different in appearance, in time the twins began to resemble each other. After decades of varying interests, involvements, motivations, their lives came to a point of intersection. They converged at an impass. Both staggered in regret behind a multiplicity of unimagined backfires. Regret fermented into chronic despair and indecisiveness. Succumbing to the vertigo of cyclic uncertainty, Doing Anything Is All Right and Doing Nothing Is All Right collapsed at an impass called nowhere.

Freedom

The cubs asked the lion whose unrivaled mane was admired far and wide: "When can we keep what's ours?"

"Keep what's ours?" the lion laughed. Come walk with me for a bit. After a scenic detailed tour of the jungle hours later they returned to where they began.

"Sit, sit." The lion said. "Curious, tired - rest but feed on these words. What's mine is mine and what's yours is mine…"

"But can't anything ever be just ours?" The whining cubs asked.

The lioness came out of nowhere, or so it seemed. With wide eyes she took all their faces in. "They asked, huh?"

"Yes, in fact I just told them that 'what's mine is mine and what's theirs is mine."

Looking at her disappointed cubs the lioness relaxed near them and clarified. "What's "yours" was "ours" to secure, defend until you could for yourself. We got, kept so you could have. Now it's your turn."

With broadening chest the lion scanned the domain then addressed his young: "A lion's heart outgrows a cub's body when first they come of age."

Surrender

Facing everything anticipating ruin	*or*	*Forging ahead in spite of temporary hazards*

MAKE A CHOICE!

Fear

Are you Facing Everything Anticipating Ruin?

If so,

Fatigue effaces accuracy rapidly

Faults eclipse ability resultantly

Flaws embed accusation resolutely

Failure empties ambition regularly

Familiarity eases anxiety radically

Finite excellence applauds relentlessly

Faith envisions adjustment redemptively

Flexibility envelops angst reassuredly

In Law

In the last bit of night before day
a badged man in blue pulled me over to say
License, insurance, registration
on Sunday 5:50am he got cooperation
His car behind, another across the street
What offense in 19° weather brought us to
    meet?
Failure to stop before turning right on red?
Thinking about it, it was just as he said
And since the old ID I forgot to replace
Two summonses would be mine to face
Police headlights shinning bright – my words
    would be few
"Happy New Year officer and God bless you.
We benefit from the law, thanks for enforcing
    it"
With hand still on his gun, what he "heard"
    was illegit

Life

Why get all upset over
what you
don't understand,
Comprehending ill timed
misfortune, doesn't come
on demand.
Violence, tsunamis,
ambition and hunger
consume
Biocide of innocence,
personhood over many
loom.
Teflon movers and
shakers
escape the bars of
reprimand,

Missed communication
indicts harmony to
isolation withstand

Would knowledge of the
tragic
euthanize its sting?

Since the wisdom, power
of prevention we don't
often bring.

Doing what we can,
accepting
what we can't maybe we
should do

But, the conclusion of
these matters is left up to
you.

Grace

*Feverishly preoccupied
with finding a remedy for
shame and insecurity, the
proud – the perfectionists
were oblivious to grace
knocking at the door.
"Please let me in, I've
brought unconditional
love to meet you."*

Voices

"Ladies and gentlemen, join me in welcoming this year's "Village Keeper," Rob Shearsome!" Thunderous applause filled the arts center as the black tie, red carpet audience affirmed the recipient. The Still I Rise choir, consisting of children with incarcerated parents, sang innocently, "Did You Ever Know That You're My Hero?;" as the honoree humbly ascended to the stage. Cameras flashed, whistles sounded as Shearsome cleared his throat to accept the prestigious award… "You are the Wind Beneath My Wings."

"Thank you! Thank you!," his bass voice offered as his hands gently bade the people to reseat themselves. "I'm honored to receive this esteemed recognition tonight and I'm grateful for the committee's selection. But more so, I'm thankful that I've been blessed by God with the opportunity to communicate hope through diverse media. Every column, infomercial, book I'VE WRITTEN"…. (HE PAUSED). THE PEOPLE RUSTLED AS Rob's voice had just gone from bass to soprano as the second syllable of "written" was pronounced. Shearsome cleared his throat and continued…

"Every column, infomercial, book I've written (perspiration had swept his calm demeanor) came from *my heart*"…pause. The soprano was exchanged for a South African tenor when "My Heart" was endearingly spoken. Stunned, the audience sat in graveyard stillness as Rob stared blankly. He wiped his mouth, forehead, loosened his bowtie and slowly tried again.

"Everything I'VE DONE that's led up to this moment…" Pause! The audience leaned forward in disbelief with quizzical looks knitting their brows. An alto with a southern drawl said the words "I've Done." Tears streamed down Rob's face. His lips quivered.

"I need to leave this award right here," he said, handing it back to the startled, ashen presenter. (The bass returned.) "It's been said that everyone is standing on somebody's shoulders. Unfortunately, I've not only used people's shoulders, but their words. Virtually all that's been attributed to me for the last 15 years came from the minds of others. I never acknowledged their material, ideas, nothing, which is now my disgrace and surely your disappointment. The irony is that tonight their voices were heard anyhow. My college English professor who gave me a love for the classics. South African leadership who refused to kneel to an unjust apartheid system. My grandmother whose maxims were more insightful than you could ever imagine. I can see her rocking on that old front porch even now."

"I guess what I'm trying to say is that instead of being a *VILLIAGE KEEPER*, I've been more like a *VILLIAGE TAKER, A THIEF.* I've plagiarized my way to acclaim. I'm sorry. Embarrassed and ashamed." With that, Rob Shearsome walked off the stage out of the light. The broadcast cut to a commercial and the show was over.

Perspective

Their hearts sank when the ominous trio entered. After hearing rave reviews about the Institute and the team in particular, the Kirby's came looking for answers. The consistent report was "First in results – last in disappointment." In spite of the playroom's appeal – Disney here, sci-fi soldiers there, slides, sinks, houses, cars, and teddy bears — a pall of desperation wrapped around them.

"Mr. and Mrs. Kirby?" A balding middle aged man wearing a Donald duck tie asked gingerly as he approached them.

"Yesssss," Mr. Kirby responded tentatively. "I'm Dr. Jacobsen. Let's sit together around the table. Thanks for coming in." Kirby and his wife loosely joined their clammy hands and walked away from the 5th floor view of autumn leaves. After being seated, with a clear view of

Mickey Mouse over Dr. Jacobsen's shoulder, they braced themselves for the worst.

"We know you're concerned about the outcome of your son's tests and our recommendations. But, first let me introduce the other members of our team. To my right, next to you Mrs. Kirby, is Brian Wells our Chaplain. To my left, next to you Mr. Kirby, is Ashley Martin, coordinator of Social Work. Not able to gather with us is Dr. Lynn Sands, psychiatrist, whom we're very honored to have join our staff at Hope's Cradle. And I'm Allan Jacobsen, pediatric neuropsychologist."

"Tell us about Parker!" Mrs. Kirby blurted. "We're absolutely baffled by his behavior. He's not like our other two. You have no idea…no idea."

Softly, Jacobsen offered: "Maybe we do have some idea… Parker's normal."

Hope

Having

Optimism

Penetrate

Evidence

MAKE IT YOUR LIFEBLOOD

The Return

From the underbelly of social blight, the fraternal twins had come. An afterthought, excused, dismissed since before they were born. Now, as sophomores in college, the inconspicuous pair spread their wings. Quickly, they dashed toward the Dean's office hoping that the brief conversation promised wouldn't eat up their time.

"You must be Tyler and Tiara. The Dean is ready to see you; go on in." The secretary then added "can I get you something?"

"No thank you" was the reply as they entered.

"Have a seat," the Dean offered. "This won't take long." With backpacks still strapped to them, Tyler and Tiara sat on the edge of the couch, side by side. Their eyes scanned the room hurriedly before settling on the Dean.

"Last weekend I met someone on the golf course who knows someone who knows you. It's a long story, but something most amazing happened. This someone who wants to remain anonymous wants to fully fund the rest of your time here. In fact, the balance of this year's tuition, room & board has already been received."

They looked at each other then back at the Dean in disbelief. Tiara spoke up "who would do that for us? Nobody like that knows us. Are you serious?"

"The person said to tell you 'every dog has it's day'"

"Nana used to say that all the time," Tyler exclaimed with a broad smile. "Maybe this someone you met knew our Nana. Maybe this is legit....So, so, how can we thank this person?" The Dean's face crawled up slowly. "I don't think that will be necessary. Tyler, Tiara I'm not sure whether I should say this or not, but "Reparation" was on the memo line of the check."

Generation to Generation

An old oak cleared its raspy throat, rustled the leaves of its sky reaching limbs and addressed the new students. "Top of the morning my young friends. I'm wise oak and I'm simply delighted to share a few thoughts with you." A dozen or so wide-eyed acorns sat up briskly waiting for more.

Wise oak continued: "Look both ways down and across the street. What do you see?" "Trees that are big like you." They shouted with joy. "Look again." "Squirrels," a few answered back. "Children," a couple of other voices chimed.

With words weighted with satisfaction, wise oak affirmed "wonderful, wonderful, and wonderful." "Now look at yourself – what do you see?" The little acorns shrugged their shoulders, sighed and pattered about. With deflated voices, they awkwardly replied: "We don't know what you mean Wise Oak. We only see who/what we are acorns." With a gentle voice that gathered the young ones around him, he offered: "so you think?"

"The big trees that line this street are what you will become. You are not just acorns. You are mighty oaks waiting to happen." The young ones looked at each other in amazement…"us, mighty oaks?"

"Yes-s-s-s, you. You are condensed potential waiting for fulfillment to break forth. That's why we're having this chat. Between what you are and what will be coming to pass, you'll encounter many things. Although squirrels will come after you, dogs will relieve themselves on you, posters will be nailed to you, winds will blow, rain will fall, ice will form, the sun will scorch, and no one may ever intentionally feed you, never forget, you are an oak! In spite of whatever… your trunk will be substantive, massive and your roots will be strong enough to buckle sidewalks. Yes, all of this will be true of you as your purpose – shade in the summer, calming color in the fall, the touch of winter's wind, and spring's sign of resilience unfolds and is occupied."

As the young ones left their mentor, almost as a chorus of whispers, they could be heard rehearsing to themselves; "Acorns for now, mighty oaks forever."

Community

*Community happens when
people interlock, realizing
that they risk being an
unsolved puzzle – an array
of pieces if they don't
choose to get together.*

Unity

Mercy Hospital Trauma Unit didn't have a minute to spare as the latest victim of gang violence was barely breathing. Officer Get It Right was combing the crime scene to find out what happened. Of course, Neutrality saw the whole thing, but as usual, knew nothing about details. "All I know is they fell out in the street." Truth in Love jumped in. "Neutrality, you know good and well it was that same gang."

Officer Get It Right cleared the air: "Just the facts, please." Truth In Love continued. "The same gang has come through this neighborhood a few times. Same gang, different day, same results. ACCUSATIONS! That's their name. They wait until you're distracted or asleep, drag you out in the street and beat you 'til you don't even know yourself."

"Did you get a look at the gang members?"

"Sure did. This time, we all got a good look. It was Insecurity, Instability, Inflexibility, with Intimidation leading. I know this may seem hard to believe, but they were all wearing the same coat – Good Intentions. They were all coated with Good Intentions."

Courage joined the conversation and put an arm around Truth in Love, who was now crying like somebody died. With a trembling voice, Courage spoke: "Officer Get It Right, whatever you do, arrest Accusation, please do it. Because what they did to Unity was horrible."

"Take heart Courage. Our Godly Sorrow Special Team knows how to handle Accusation."

Four days later, Destiny, Unity's sibling, flew in on eagles' wings. Startled to find Unity coherent after such a public whipping, the doctor was asked what happened… "Last night, half asleep, half awake, Unity faintly whispered: 'Father forgive…Lord Jesus save us all…I choose not to be offended.' That little prayer started the change."

Celebration

"Good morning everyone. Hope the weekend agreed with you. I thought we'd look today at "celebration." What have your experiences of celebration been? What was celebrated? How was it celebrated? Make a few notes around the celebrations that stand out, that come first to mind."

"Oh that's easy, birthdays". Leon exclaimed. We rotated an everybody's birthday party.

Candace asked: "What do you mean? I'm not following this rotation thing."

Leon explained: "Well, one year the party was in February, because that's when my birthday is. Another year, it was in June because that's when my brother's is and so on. When the birthday party fell in your month, then you got to decide one activity for the celebration. A second activity was always decided on by the rest of the family. One year, we went skiing; another year, we had a block party. It's always a good time."

Alexander jumped in: "What about your parents? Are their birthdays part of this cycle of celebration?"

"Yeah. Why wouldn't they be?" Leon responded in absolute puzzlement.

Alexander shifted in his seat, scratched his head and said (more to himself than to the class) "whole family celebrates their birthdays together at one time and rotates when that happens…hmmm."

"Speak up Alexander. We can't hear you," the teacher called as though trying to reel something back in that's about to get away.

Now, fully audible, Alexander continued. "Never mind. I was just trying to get with Leon's rotating birthday celebration. At our house, we went out to dinner and could take a friend with us. Gifts came too. Individually, we celebrated individually, nothing really out of the ordinary. Graduations were big events though. Family, friends would get together the night before to hear the graduate's dream list. From that point on, somebody would always ask for a "dream update!" I just heard from my uncle last week. "Boy, how's that dream coming? A mixed up world like this needs somebody like you. Keep at it.

"This is all sooo strange," Candace blurted, as she shook her head back like a rock star and put her hair behind her ears. "Everything was soo different at our house. We had so many celebrations, it's like gridlock in my mind trying to figure out what stands out, because they all do at the same time. She glanced quickly at the list of jubilation before her. "There was potty training…."

"Potty Training?", Leon shouted, as the rest of the class burst into laughter.

"Let's get some respect going here," the teacher said, trying to refocus the group. (Although she was as struck at the words as they were.) "Go on Candace."

"I don't know what's so funny. It's true," she offered innocently. "We celebrated potty trainings, riding bicycles without those little wheels, cheerleading, driving permits, all kinds of stuff." By now, a veil of amazement trimmed in disbelief had come over the seminar group. Oblivious to it, Candace continued. "Our first dates turned into real bashes when we got home. It was sooo much fun. I, mean, we did the regular birthdays, anniversaries, holidays, but sooo much more. Everything was special at our house."

"I'm not so sure about that." Alexander said, as though walking on egg shells. "If everything is special, how can anything be special?"

"What do you mean?", Candace asked, as though something foreboding might be waiting ahead.

Alexander pushed his chair back from the circle, shook his head and closed his laptop. "Never mind Candace. You wouldn't get it. You're already pouting."

An awkward 30 seconds or so snailed by. The clock was looked at, nails tapped on the desk, soda sipped. Leon broke the silence. "Brianna, how about you? You haven't said anything."

"There's not too much to say", she replied, looking embarrassed and extremely uncomfortable. "Whenever we tried to do holidays, some argument, fight would usually break out. It was guaranteed that somebody's feelings would get hurt. I guess what stands out is that we survived our celebrations. (pause) You know there was something that stood out. My grandfather was drunk and told us he loved us. Usually, he'd park himself in front of the TV, watch the game and that was it. You couldn't bother him. You know, he always kept to himself. But that year was different. (Tears began to trickle down her face.) He had too much to drink. Pop grabbed us one by one, kissed us and said "I love you." Seems like I can still smell the alcohol on his breath and feel that sloppy kiss marking me."

"Drunk or sober, it's the love that keeps it real." Leon announced as he leaned forward. "That's what I'm taking about, the love thing."

Alexander responded: "that village thing is on my mind. I'm trying to pull it up. You know the one I mean,…" as he snapped his fingers. "How does it go…?"

"Oh, 'it takes a whole village to raise a child'?" The teacher suggested.

"No. That's good but that's not it… what is it? What is it?....Oh, I got it! 'I am because we are.' That's what I was trying to think of. What do our celebrations have to do with us as individuals and us as a part of the village? Where does the village come in?"

Candace snapped with attitude. "What do you mean village? My potty training, cheering parties were mine, for me. Just like my brother's stuff was all for him and my sister's for her. What was mine was mine. "Only mine!"

"Yeah and I bet every other week something was all somebody's in your house. Bells, whistles, chips, ice cream, whatever – it was all for you or for them," Brianna interrupted.

"How did you know?"
Candace replied like a deer in headlights.

"We can tell Candace it doesn't take much to see it."

"Okay group, that's all for today. Our time is up. Next class we'll pick up with this same question: "Can a celebration be for me and for us at the same time?" The teacher stated.

"What do you mean 'for me – for us' at the same time?" Candace questioned.

Alexander spoke. "Candace when you catch on to this 'for me – for us' thing we'll all celebrate."

Overheard

I'll be so glad when I can talk again. How long has it been? The days have rolled into weeks, maybe months by now, I'm not sure. It's taken a while – or so it seems just to be able to think. My body feels like its trying to wake up. This buried under sand feeling is too much. It's just too heavy…maybe that's a good sign. Maybe actually being able to sense something like weightiness is a sign that my brain and my body are coming back to life. I hope before the day is out, I'll be able to let someone know, in a way that they can understand that I'm alive.

My hearing has been holding its own all along. That will come as a surprise to many. Well, that is, if I tell them. No, I don't think I want to remember everything that was whispered, mentioned, discussed, prayed and overheard. – (I wish I could reach for a tissue or pull this sheet up since my tear ducks are working overtime.) I'm not sure I even know what to do with the words that were actually spoken to me instead of over me. No, I can't carry all they said when they didn't know I was listening. This is upsetting. I better try and calm myself, a nap. Let me try to nap. Let me try to walk the beach or something. Hear the ocean's wave as the sun is glistening a good morning…

(Two Days Later) Thank you Jesus! I was finally able to get an "uh huh" out. As soon as I can write again, I'm going to send a letter in reference to that nurse. She's always talked to me like I was still a real person. Everyday approaching me like she expected something good, no matter how small, to happen – 'Well, hello; can you blink for me today? Move a finger, a toe, foot. Just try for me.' And today was Yes! the day something happened. A little sound and a little movement happening on the same day. I'm on my way!

(Two hours later) I wonder if they're going to send someone to officially see if I can talk, a speech therapist or something. I can't wait until the doctor comes. Maybe I'll practice what I want to say to him. Yeah. That will do. I'll practice what I want to say to him as well as the regulars who come in. Probably, I should say less than what I'm actually thinking so I don't wear myself out. Aside from that, I don't know if I can deal with it. A set back is the last thing I need, especially one caused by hearing my own self…Settled. I'll practice a few words and those will have to speak the volumes that will be left unsaid.

(Three hours later) His smile was encouraging. I didn't know a simple "yes" or "no" could bring a smile to a doctor's face. That was nice. I'm glad I could get those two little words out. Well, I can try them out again if visitors come. Why am I saying if? When they come is what I should say. Let me think this through. Since I already decided that the fewer words the better, what would I like to say and what will I really try to say!

Let's see…For those who started being present "in spirit" more often than in body, who fumbled with excuses for why they couldn't make it after all, so they sent an 'I love you' by someone else, I'd like to say don't send your love. It loses something when it's packaged in excuses. I know you're overwhelmed. Stay home without guilt. Your reaction to what you've seen when you've looked at me breaks me down on the inside. Your visits probably aren't helping either one of us. That's what I'd like to say. But what I will say is: "Don't Worry."

For those who have been here like clock-work, I'd like to say you stepped in possibly because you thought "nobody" else would. Whether by default or out of compassion, you rearranged your lives to be here. Don't come every day like you don't have a life of your own. 'Do something else in the evening without guilt. You're tired. I can hear it in your voice. That's what I'd like to say. But what I will say is: Thank you.

For those who never came because they "just couldn't take it," I'd like to say what you couldn't take, I didn't have the option not to. When it dawned on me that I never heard your voice, I felt alone. Where were you?! That's what I'd like to say. But what I'll say is … What I'll say is… I guess I don't know yet. I guess for right now it doesn't matter. Unless they hear something about me that they can "take" and come up here sooner than later.

Phew, I'm tired now. Coming back to life is hard work.

*A pearl is the gift of
sustained frustration …
Chronic irritation
can be transformed into
something of beauty.*

TAKE HEART!

After Words

Many threads make a garment so also the encouragement, effort, listening, and prayers of others made what you're now reading possible. Their commitment, time energy, interest, service, were primary invaluable strands. Special people indeed – they know who they are. Thanks for all that you do over and over again.

Consistently contributing to the shape of my life have been some choice long-term relationships. (i.e. Betsy Morgan, who was my English Professor in college). They know who they are and how glad I am that we've sojourned on this side of eternity. Thanks for being who you are.

Finally, I'm grateful to God the communicating, relational, Ultimate Designer - Sustainer of Life including mine.

While wearing this garment of communal support and sitting at the kitchen table with Josiah whispers were overheard. Thanks for listening.

To God be the Glory!

Reflection Questions

Awakening

The Score
- How do you define love?

The Mirror
- What gets in your way of reflection?

The Twins
- What is it to just be?
- What is the mantra of "All Right"?

Freedom
- What does courage mean to you?
- How do you participate in others "coming of age"?

Surrender

In Law
- Write a story of when you misperceived someone's intention.
- Write about a time when someone misrepresented your intention.

Life
- What do you do when a tsunamis comes in your life?

Grace

Voices
- Who has influenced you and is unacknowledged?
- Who received awards?

Perspectives
- Recall a time when you thought your mind was absolutely made up about something and you had a change of perspective.

Hope

Return
- Describe a gift you'd like to receive without strings?
- When was the last time something unexpected happened in your life?

Generation to Generation
- Identify the wise oaks in your life and how these wise oaks helped your purpose come to pass?
- "Acorns for now, mighty oaks forever." What positive affirmations can you practice?

Community

Unity
- How does neutrality impact community?
- When have you chosen not to be offended?

Celebration
- What was blocking Candace's experience of "we?"

Overheard
- "Coming back to life is hard work." What needs to be resuscitated in you?

<u>Note:</u> Mental health professionals Charlesetta T. Sutton, MSW, LCSW and Karen D. Wells, Psy.D provided questions for reflection.

Index

Community

in the kitchen with Josiah

the author.

daughter, sister, friend, minister, colleague, student, teacher, neighbor, listener, i am grateful clay and a Christian gladly.

b.g.

CPSIA information can be obtained at www.ICGtesting.com
260130BV00002BA/1/P